MW01268841

bk of (h)rs

bk of (h)rs

⤝ *Pattie McCarthy* ⤞

APOGEE PRESS

BERKELEY, CALIFORNIA

2002

acknowledgements

Sections of/excerpts from this poem first appeared in the following: *The American Poetry Review: Philly Edition 99, The Boston Review, The East Village Web, Facture, ixnay magazine, Kenning, murmur, Outlet, Poets & Poems* on the St. Mark's Poetry Project Website, *The Portable Boog Reader, Tool, The Transcendental Friend,* and *The Washington Review.* My thanks to the editors for their support & kindness. For reading this poem & for offering generous insight, I am grateful to Marcella Durand, Kristin Prevallet, Heather Ramsdell, & Karen Weiser.

Thanks are also due to the many sources, from the eleventh century to the present one, to which this poem is indebted.

Thank you (for everything)
Jenn McCreary, Carol Mirakove,
Cole Swensen, & Kevin Varrone.

COVER IMAGE: "*Marie Magdaleine coppe ses cheveux et offrit contrition.*" From the 14th-century *Livre de la Passion.* Vatican City, Biblioteca Apostolica Vaticana.

BOOK DESIGN: Philip Krayna Design, Berkeley, California. www.pkdesign.net

ISBN 0-9669937-7-2. Library of Congress Catalog Card Number 2001-135180.

Published by Apogee Press
Post Office Box 8177
Berkeley CA, 94707-8177
www.apogeepress.com

I wille make all thynge wele, I shall make all thynge wele,
I maye make alle thynge wele and I can make alle thynge wele.
—JULIAN OF NORWICH, *Shewings*

-<← bell (h)rs →>-

matins *1*

blue, then. again she is—bending. against
a gilt-checked backdrop, palm fronds.
there is the denial of the senses & then
there is the obliteration thereof. she came
back to life with the relics of sweat on her
tongue & strips of fretting fabric,
something you lost unrecognizable in her
hands. textile fragment :
       removed for restoration.
suspended & broken folds of her mantle.
to cover, to cast off.
given   that   we   will   re-assemble
given that we will pass things without notice
: a torso from a deposition, given its posture
: a series of heads in profile encircled
by a tendril meander.
the more—the more—the more—your
unlimited cache of rapt faces.
so   give   me   something
to   cover   my   eyes.
all open doors are nervewracking.

all the makings : the bones of a saint, black
shoes on the bedspread. reliquaried your
weight, a fall of hair. she's gone to ground
& found the hive. they were, of course, all
necessarily   sometimes   daughters.
that desire should be relinquished
upon the veil.
the clerestory as choice & not-choice.
alphabetically I was a cinch & cut
you out from the philosophy.
"(instrument) for taking the stars"
that kind of singlemindedness
smacks of bad behavior kept behind teeth.
all these things are one day sore. here
where everything is rolling out from green,
as if you could find a central spot, to still be
still. the other green was reached crushing
new wild violets & mixing massicot.
something you lost & the manner
in which it is lost. & so your eyes are
painted the color of a dark coat at night,
frantic with absence & struck by return. or
should I say, struck with realization of it.
shall we meet in the after ?
some strange comfort, such as it is.

lauds

sometimes the city is there, sometimes
it is only fashioned there, & sometimes
one cannot make anything of it.
if there's a distance, console me with that
it's always equal.
what isn't worth having or pinches
limits. anyone who grew up behind
the wreckage of a pastoral screen door.
the eccentric treatment of the heads : low
foreheads & emphatic eyes. attenuated
in high relief : linear treatment of drapery &
the agitated, fluttering hemline. she has this
distinction : burned one june thirteen-ten,
some   years   after   her   book   :
       & what could she be given ? if she
       were given all that ever has been
       given & shall be given, this would
       be nothing in comparison
hover, how I envy you that.
       : the shrines tumbled, lamps pale
                      (an omen—)

when a streetlight burns out as one passes
(that happened several times last night).
the candle as jester : the book, the bell—
they will say it as though a shirt pushed
up   over   the   ribcage.   as   though   so
      simply breakable : now
make that true again.
he answered—the girl will catch
an apple with the lap of her skirt.
the three of them, a gaggle of homonyms,
conceived & carved as a single
element within the drama of the scene.
judging from my jaw, I dreamt
bare & nervous. her only chronology
given to us by these two burnings.
your name has become a beautiful excuse
at the top of the page. aspersions & the like
cast. yet all are in fine fettle. said as though
we   met   with   our   mouths.
as in to sharpen : from the needle. an ounce
long pepper & one of tumeric, two ounces
grains of paradise & the same of steel filings
all in a powder—an electuary with honey &
taken about the size of a walnut. at night
         & morning. good morning.

prime

ash is not a solid.
in the course of awake—take
a wineglass of this decoction : garden rue
& wormwood, horehound & the finest
nettles : for some days.
bleuet has set a feast of sorrows
& all our humors in a row—
in that dress that doesn't suit me & is
incapable of my own distress or your
life spent in hallways.
the reconciliation of reason with revel
is drenched, an arras : weather & equinox.
largely forgotten like fine lettering
& whirligigs. fine things in general.
wanting them to converge :
          they do not converge.
hindered by her own mercy—he
does not carry his learning as lightly.
the alphabet borrowed & re-arranged
when I learned the puzzle of spelling
          vertebræ : something to turn on.

his physics a religion without
narrative : etymology a science
they thought we put too much stock in.
what I mistranslated as *how you changed*
truly reads *have you (an)other*—I have
something to say about pot-metals
& declension.
if this is sinking, darling—then
          sink it is & so we shall.
matches run low—avoid this by keeping
candles lit. the process can also be
counted upon to process. on 'don't walk'
we stop—too much of you
falls   about   my   head.
"logic has made me hateful" he said & he
was correct.
now, he is an infant. later, he will be dead.
these are the given continental options.
there will be lovers & subterfuge
there will be deaths of circumstance
& spectacle. there will be three
intermissions. she said *pietà* & she said it
siccus oculis. I dreamt I spoke in my sleep
—but I do not. a disgruntled orchestra
enters a traffic circle.

terce

they hand it out & we take it
because it is given.
I have taxed the imaginary you
to its dissolution.
groan is akin to grin; sigh is unattested.
again, there are three & they are linked
each to the other & to their book
with an interchange of color & aerial
perspective. again, there are three in her
digression. not what thing
is experienced but how somesuch thing
is experienced. of late.
we would do well to consider this.
there will be no intermission
& the knowledge of this is the crux.
all that time spent in train stations—those
timetables kept, his every & only one.
he met every train & I envied him that.
his eve is prone—
but pleasant enough
looking & on her belly among

seedlings. the only surviving & broken
bit of this particular tympanum. he left
a signature—which is considered unusual.
she was made similar to ether.
: in fact, whenever one has a hoarse voice
      without any infirmity, they have
      secrets & are hence
      shrewd. but if this throat is forced
      somehow to give clear sound
: that person will die soon.
tears for a fiddler
            similar to ether
the eye is composed of fire & water.
the eye is dark off-shore & always at night.
his eve is her contemporary & the word
she used was "ensnare"—partly hidden
but almost swimming & about to speak.
or whisper. which, via
an old & dubious etymology,
brings us again to sigh
(which you insist is an exquisite dessert).
there is an impossibly high white staircase
which dominates centerstage :
& someone will surely climb it
& will climb it more than once.

sext

that the vertebræ are each small skulls—
a ladder of stones or a ladder
whose footholds are each a maw in every
bone. the river felt
    she wanted salt.
both a choice & the thing chosen.
in folklore, it delivers drops of poison.
it is a columnar assemblage; it is a slender
axis for larger, spinning mechanisms.
what it does it does and does by rote.
here are three more, the colors typically
subdued in deference, saffron & rose : tea
impatiently steeped & strawberry-rhubarb.
here, there are three : splintered & blunt-
forged with which he will be redeemed
for reaching. the background composed of
a rather somber berry-maroon
overlaid with leaves in almost hysterical
swirling patterns. a simple sky
would be inappropriate,
given what follows.

I get everywhere by rote—
hardly noticing shops or corners,
wishing for a letterbox
version of life or for one
large enough for books. this
isn't a lot to ask. something has scratched
your name in my eye.
they are called "scintillating"
sometimes they are called
"fortification spectra" since
their margins appear furnished with turrets
or battlements of a fashion.
note her vision of extinguished stars.
these were migraines or prescience.
an invitation to make
something productive from the ritual
residue
kept under our tongues, surreptitiously.
mostly not noticing these are ember days.
he had not known such music
existed. thereafter, he heard it everyday.
the way they've displayed his ribs
can only be described as panicked.
my peripheral
vision catches the world behind me.

we un-did the vernacular & un-hitched
                    the pluvious debris.
                    the grief has aged
her by this page. a brutal grisaille
disproportionate to a reach misunderstood
as a loving gesture. or, at the very least,
an arm outstretched intending no harm.
"(plant with) footlike leaves" whose pulp
is edible but its single, nodding flower is
poisonous. its dried
resin is cathartic & their faces
are monochromatic in grizzled caterwaul.
her arm, the length of everything intended
nothing. meant nothing in its own context.
reached *toward*—extended into
consequence
which had little to do with her arm, its
length—chiselled
out from one another & yet still one
another—yet still intertangled,
pulling weeds from the neck of my sweater.

should we return, we would not recognize
ourselves without the colors.
we would be stunned & perhaps
dismayed at how we've faded.
at a certain point in that particular century
(& ever since), her arms were raised.
cinnabar, a single embellishment in its
severity—everything   draws   away
from   &   pushes   us   to   the   disaster
                    : resembling an almost total
                    eclipse, fourteen - oh - six.
we know how to make leap-years
now—we think we know how to
account for nonsense reckonings.
we know how to make shadows
where the earth is warm—
we know to hang copper pots above hot
vinegar, to further dissolve it in wine : all
sorts   of   temperas   were   devised.
their bodies produce
no sound in motion.
early winter pulls the rings from our fingers.
there's an element of quid pro quo to this
that leaves one kneeling & baffled as to why
: the gesture is addictive, is catching.

vespers

it was correct to refer to words as voices—
when the visual was not necessarily initial.
our most minimal exchanges.
in a chronological row of vesperbilds,
her cryings
become more calm, sucessively
subtler lamentations.
& there is keening, as usual—folding
the torso toward earth, still partly fastened.
if so much had been given,
          much was expected.
the revision as suspect as the original.
consider the evidence of our eyes : scores
will be settled inevitably & irrevocably.
the gaggle swoons to see it; look to her,
          look to her,   look to her.
diagonal vaults on the useful nightstairs.
twenty-four thousand one hundred & six
ritual lines on my distaff side.
one hundred & seventeen chapters
devoted to silence.

an early equinox, counted backwards from
fixed feasts—elimination of ten *real* days.
retroactive adjustment v. astronomical
accuracy. this unwillingness to be arbitrary.
a complicated system of thrust &
counterthrust. or, rather, an unwilling
admission to necessary arbitrariness.
I could have shorn my head, stuck pins
in it. or rubbed my lips with quicklime.
here : a septet. all but one exist as comfort
to, as adjunct to her stricken & small figure.
& that one takes her drastic place like an
arcanum. she is downstage & dressed in
spun sugar. (we have no way to reason
these perfectly sound rules for blue
that result in rose.)
I forgot myself;
I lost track of my cold fingers.
there can be too much to say—so
that we mostly ignore the thing itself.
a requisite quietus before sleep.
an unusual subject, an inventory of limbs.
& we can certainly scramble : to get it all
in, to force it all out, to speak. to allow for
the possibility that someone told the truth

compline

it is maddening : to understand the math
of it; to feel fingers stretch to it—but
never able to execute it in fact.
remove the tough center rib & chop
the kale fine.   made similar.
your name is on my desk somewhere—
     (transfixed by arrows, it is familiar)
it is the lesser; it is selfless in its kitchen.
given my spectacles, precipitation.
mediate between unruly etyms & intention
so that we can admit to being human,
volatile, & glottal.
: in flight,
rotating postures contrast static. her dress
a vertical buttress. it turned his head, it did.
motions only obvious in reverse.
oddly, she was
condemned with excerpts.
the final consonant became mute early (see
lamb), but never accurately mimicked
pronunciation. nonetheless, it is accepted.

that we should make an effort at all those
letters : their affectionate obligations.
had they lips or hands, perfectly still or
a noise created by quarter notes.
the necessary spices—we knew this
was coming. she has handed them over.
she has changed her dress & taken on
the expected gesture.
something more to say about despair : her
upturned face & a fissure in the landscape,
the return of the sky. a fragment of reversal
marked by implied resignation.
where he relies on renunciation—her
emphasis on intensification of the ordinary,
& gradually. as though nothing
miraculous is underfoot.
motions too slow to notice.
in a later book, they will choose to reveal
her face clearly, a guilty impersonal patina.
stove-lit, a tea tin with your evening in it.
streetlights throw haloes down around the
lampposts, a tattooed lens refractive defect.
sixteen violins, our broken sentences.
we insist on seeing
them with our dim eyes.

‹‹ (p)salter ››

.i

losing piano : : wall of windows,
this is a glass door. unstrung his
is evidently suitable—
       wings   affixed   with   a   shrug
       wings   alight   on   pins   & needles
counting off against
the   thumb,   a   measure   for   nothing—
index, third, ring, fifth.
this instrument, with regards
to its overstrings & hammers,
is descendant. it is the stitch when
       it is badly sewn.

.ii
juli/an : :

§2451728   how he knows tonight
there will be deer in the road.
it would be pretty to think. if Socrates
had been a starling—what alomancy
                    : my mouth is
enlarged over mine enemies.

a sad plaster of paris statue, cracked
fairy lights, roadside votaries.
a garden enclosed is
my sister—doves, in reality, do not hover.
hawks & larks do, however.
ave eva, a drop of the oceansize.
these songs & others : I caught
all of these songs from you.
uncorrupted   (from scratch to ash that is)
she was invented in the fifth century.
          the quarterly triple-witching
          purging herself thirty-six handed
          chickens in lieu of a canary

the story is said to be apocryphal, but
all the same it's true—the sorrows
officially fixed at seven. & one prodigy
awkwardly
pulling her knees to her chest, just
          twisted, her neck—
in the miracle plays, when an actor
lay down & died, a bird was pulled
upward by a sting.   somewhere
I have ever been
          "far-nigh"

§2451738   bells are rung, given
the month & thunder what hope can
there be for corn ? this peculiar incomplete
mastery of perspective makes for an icon
rather like staring down a squinch.
                    green how much
I want written brittle over—his ellipticism
is an improvement upon the subject.
too much of your
face falls about me
amongst much speculation & under
much weight, without any accuracy.
I am guiltless of precision. nonetheless,
that's one impressive handkerchief.
the stance immobile to maneuver it
slowly before the charge.
the inevitable presence of a suspended
          spindle (with bent fingers,
a fork & card) : crushing flax—the process
can be counted on to never cease.
retting, hackling, retting, pirn in a gyre.
is surrendered upon a veil.
a decorative cluster of speedwell
makes you a rebus. & traces your name &
image back into nothing.

§2451746   in a book today
our former street
was an alley & giving chase & all
the alleys arterial to it
listed & given as escapes. & I was sad
         : the map is not the territory.
indeterminate. we would recognize
it as lanugo. but a diagnosis at this
distance is dubious, to say the least.
comely, uncumber
in very sharp vinegar   seven   whole
eggs   until softened to the likeness
of thin skin   mix with four ounces
dried mustard & anoint   frequently.
also of things : to act as a cog or restraint.
to load or fill (places, things) with what
is obstructive, useless.
⸮ to fold (the arms) obsolete

         she confides forties of Solomon
         silver turned to water in his hands

§2451748 she is collaged
c. the turn of the seventh.
the ogive is a hypocrite—stasis & balanced
on absence, simultaneous cause & effect.
            (she raises a jar & asks are those
            my teeth chattering ? I am dead)
figures from the verso bled through,
so they appear to be watching
her from a distance.
again, her hair is an issue. its removal.
too many, because we are.
            their cryings
            their embrace (like lovers)
in order to make the translation
he bit out a piece of her arm.
the 'turn' with the doubter in juxtaposition
was meant to diminish.

a map of shifting attitudes
a golden head upon a litter
a thin excuse to paint nudes

the columns believe
they are forcing the ribs upward
& the ribs believe
they are holding the columns down.
vice versa—there is no v.v.
a fixture
a tower
a ladder in the firmament c. the circus
say 'burning burning' for the easy laugh

each of these
three marys, in single-file, line me up.
            the gesture is catching
            an episodic
representation : she is reading; over
her left shoulder, the three of her
are making a discovery; there is a jar.
"I ran
all the way here to tell you this."
sentences
as the disiecta membra of other sentences.

more a merger than an invention proper—
in eleven-oh-five : polysemy
three to equal one
& that one
truly a fourth thing in itself
          tessera
          tessaraic (after mosaic)
maybe it isn't as much fun as one would
initially suppose being coined as a word.
                    (we hold empty names)
predella : I am sorry; I am a hermit;
I am modestly clothed
mostly in my own neglect.
: no more of her than the skull,
          the feet & the palms of her hands.
: a book, keys, a rudderless boat,
          a sunbeam in clear water.
"I ran all the way here to tell you this."
the jar is misunderstood. something
woeful about becoming
a sentimental adjective.   a flourish on
a heretical apprentice pillar. red letter days
when I mistook the word 'bird' for bird.
since south & noon cannot be
distinguished from one another.

.iii

spinning-jenny : : arrive
widdershins, but return
                    deasil—
no more free of that than
the quag or the curlew, are you ? in babel
captive; of the clavichords at the met :
painted behind the strings; of window
quarrels : a spider hidden in a nutshell.
a query mistranslated to secure a given
answer. during the fourth night-watch
the *aster* of disaster :
            if yet not, after

.iv

syllabus of errors : : loved bells. lived for forty days on air sipped from a spoon. believed salamanders to be impervious to fire. danced the fandango dressed in silver scales. disguised instability as principle. developed a terror of ice. buzzed low notes. mashed potatoes. wanted to go home & shut the door. feared the subway. loved the ritual. wore khakis. kept an unruly household. heard voices. imagined them. lied. received gifts & performed the requisite obligations. refused to speak. married. understood causality. made unnecessary intercessions. considered cleverness a weapon. distrusted veneration & unreasonable enthusiasm. grew impatient. recanted for fear of the stake. relapsed. desired authenticity— not in the scholarly sense. studied the principles of good stained glass. converted clovis. cried before bed. preferred not to. sang before supper. became unreasonably enthusiastic. thought meditation might help. thought medication might help. swallowed thistles & thorns. knew pretty teeth to be the ruin of pretty eyes. preferred sitting to prostitution. believed the devil collected slurred syllables in a sack. tied knots in the belts of dead men. lit candles & shut up the dogs. took walks. discussed the shape of genius. relied on the sympathetic influence of the clavicle. invented barbed wire. cried poverty. would not budge an inch for all the idiocies of this world. heard voices. denied them. lied. spun sugar. did not trust gravity. recognized the names of only three. recommended tolling bells against a storm. always withdrew by walking backwards. spun flax. crushed velvet. knew careless utterances to have consequences. exhibited traditional expressions of grief such as setting hair on fire. stopped answering the phone. attributed deep motives to the most trivial actions. slept naked on spiny twigs. spent nine years jumping out of windows. had screaming fits & fell down, in phases. fasted. lived without water for a month. chewed on lemon seeds. did not swallow them. lingered. starved to death. anticipated encounters with wax. made proclamations. became weary of them. feared unread books. named names. made the index.

.v

orison / (horizon) is laid
flat : appearing, as it does.
there's no way to start

this slowly. if you die, then we all do.
one cautionary denominator.
monastic again as adjectival

clutter. a collection : senseless
misnomers, caught unprepared.
furta sacra—*its* and *thems*.

salt and distracted, to drag it out.
thoroughly wrought : the thing
is magic, unimaginable.

that was someone falling : once
asked, there's no retrieving it.
that syllable drops into hostile

genuflection. to never begin
anything in grief again.
this evening was a masterpiece

indeed. the greediness
of it, its placement on the tongue :
antiphon. I'm aware of the changing

shape of my eyes, by hairlines.
a cauldron of bellies, legs
meeting under a barstool. my own

recently the more given.
your narration in reprisal
is reversible. unpedestalled, still

illusory : *the last sad office*
pay. I think of how we might
simply walk out.

the syntax of the miraculous that
comes to pass at night, comes to characterize.
what we get as wholly unexpected.

the sum of my education, that
music the more brutal.
therefore or rather your sometimes sister.

.vi
(h)rs for Paris use : : I admire your reluctance
to accept time as an abstract; your daylight
savings opposition; your talent for descending
dark banister-less stairs. everything
pragmatic is divided by six.
all these chimneys—& not one that smokes.
it's disconcerting.
though it is no
        less   numinous.   inadvertent   errors   may   have   crept   into   this   text.
in the meantime, musicians nod to each   structure
other—the cue to begin across
the nave & other rooms, across the city, from
one smug string to the nesting collarbones.
& the way she turns her head aside
accommodates both the audience & cello.

I'm bored with wishing you well.
the building empties on a square & signal
from the bells & there's nothing like a mass
                    to make you want one.
the cupped hands & forward
shoulders give everything away.
so I recognize &
            appreciate the gesture.
it's not suspect like so many
things we do with our hands & glances.
at breakfast, with a language barrier.
under these circumstances I should
perhaps be holding a poppy, or making
more of an effort with my hair.
a translation of days—so that our footsteps fall synchronized on the hill rather than
the weeks & years & countless names between the action & contact. leaving me
feeling more julian than gregorian & thus confused.
under these circumstances it occurs.

the second letters of the original seven
antiphons read backwards yield the acrostic :
I shall be with you tomorrow.
divinations to undertake—times
& purposes to be determined regionally.
I'm not one for a public shrove. *confessions of sins <Ash Wednes>*
a green winter makes for a fat churchyard. *thankful*
a long winter makes for a full ear. poke *complaints*
      holes in eggshells to keep   > *superstition*
        witches from going to sea. we look down into it.
it is forbidden to make miracles in lieu so the ecstatic girls quit their meowing.
the thing is impossible. you compel
each breath to sound
regular & the muscles
climb our arms.
the forced bulbs are slightly obscene
& make me so, unlikely.
this has been our lot since pigeon domestication, since
it's one of the perils of our subway line
     : for we are, needless to say, in a skull, but I have no choice but to add the following
few remarks. I am looking for a suitable hat in the rain.

         ↳ *something to protect*

coffee against another crenellated headache; skulking
against that encumbering annunciated yellow till
there's no corner left.
looking more bemused than terrified
or honored at the prospect
          : through & over the whole set another theme "goes" but it is not played.
if it exists, it has never been established.
perhaps all would have been well had she
stuck to bric-a-brac; turned her
talents to knick-knacks. a theory of drapery—
seeing things to scale.
we like to think of marble as variable.
ropes of sand & sea-slime—
          (leading nowhere)
unfledged minions flaunting it.
                    didn't I bring precious gifts ? despite reason,
despite your education in this wise—aren't you pained to see
the gallery stripped bare ?
                              three words, it was said,
would suffice & she delivered herself of six hundred.
a fragment dispersed. you, trees, a lamppost, a bridge,
the river—so many delightful right angles in view.
plaques on beautiful houses cuing : nothing happy happened here.
in the *kay* v. *key* debate, I keep my mouth shut. like with *bourgeoisie*—it's better avoided.

throw confetti, old woman.

rustic & illogical—is anything better, or worse, than a mile ?

those that refuse to go barefoot or take oaths, apparently.

it's tragic as it is static, as it's a mirror

that flatters—we cannot discuss

this question with your mouth

full of fig. ⟶ *lies*

they are among the more deceptive fruits.

the awful dissolution of joints & limbs—

     (there was no break in the skin).

there's no one in it but ourselves.

the objection to things

broken into parts is foundation of so much superstition.

begghini combusti : as the body in some conceptual

fragmentation was much feared—

thoughts are connected by *and* & *then*

    instead of being subordinated to each other; aggregated rather than analytic.

clumped so can't pick out real meaning

like the corbeling we were pleased to find

making dark & make-believe the alleys that once

ran down into river but are now bolstered by

said quays.

I number none but

shining—   gravelblind.

to know by fixed stars, to turn inequal to equal, to know southly.

figs with salted water & sour syrup will rid you of gravel & sediment.
for an otherwise effect : "crater" each fig with cinnamon, salt, & basil.
I knew a joke once about a chicken for Chaucer's kitchen
            & another about this street, rotisserie, & Hugo.
sympathetic menus, other such palaver
            (a word I only hear in your italics).
break into vernacular to characterize desire—this is the thing
in depositions, a central axis
will be formed from nails after
the body is removed.
as when scoliosis was the disease célèbre & all that adolescence was bustled up in metal.
as opposed to the hips & bellies
protruding in gothic portrait martyrologies—it's the same
exact slant
cultivated now. that slow choreographic walk : how much
it has in common with their disinterested
            looks, their boyish slouching.
                  : paint her
                     eyes dark then.
do I know you ? indeed, & we exchanged each for each on nonsuch street.
kept the books & the mathematics of our visit.

we are not to meet here, but elsewhere. vowels,
but particularly dipthongs, conspire to give history
away & I round them, lilt balloons despite
my best efforts. is that effort ? is that
sense of falling upward true—it can
not be true. what is it about that corner ?
two
sounds now pronounced
singularly. : I'll have your head upon a platter have you up against the wall.
not one new word today, a failure.
no resolution regarding the imaginary child or the hypothetical leaky
warehouse roof, not a failure. it's
the great vowel shift c. twelfth
                                    cigarette dinnertime. in the year of nostalgic cellar
wartime American swing. speaking of
the war, which we do, it's yet another archaic justification for eastern DST, say you
: vir dolorum—misthink delirium
which has nothing to do with nothing herein.

& writing after. & isn't it
all after. what were once day's eyes. made useless by geography—
I threw quarters at your window; lacked sufficiently romantic
gestures & the word for that area
between the scapulæ.
& after : a bath or false
                                    memoir, merging 'travel' & 'error' in the nave for a wild-haired
conductor, wiry creatures
suspended by invisibles. drag a bow across anything gut tonight.
absurd, regardless—I cannot bring myself to use another
woman's wooden spoon, totem-
burned, knotted not at all unlike.
                    a   wonder   at   bog   Latin   &   broke   it   against   the   roof   of   my   mouth.
altered as though through metempsychosis or linseed until
another. a measure for nothing, a glottal stop.

↤ bk of (h)rs ↦

Sometimes that's how it is, in a way, the eyes take over, and the silences, the sighs, like the sighs of sadness weary with crying, or old, that suddenly feels old and cries for itself, for the happy days, the long days, when it cried it would never perish, but it's far from common, on the whole.
—SAMUEL BECKETT, *Texts for Nothing*

To Sophia and Isabella

a sudden light, so they say (you said "sudden" like "southern")—or moment, that blink, illogical to the last eyelash. dissolves into mythos. dame street : an alley acoustic, a front step mosaic. under construction—jackhammer accompaniment, foreign sirens. let's order the moonshine. at sunset or high tide—or both I can't remember : that night you swallowed her tongue for me. "the past is a grasshopper." the curve of a shadow lunches on a marble stoop, the alley exhausts hair as fences fall into doubling. flutter of schoolchildren explode onto a lawn. setting. vowels heaped like terrorism. here we mean tourism. fifty pages in the garbage. a moment ? no, a moment is a pinprick. let's be suspicious, very suspicious, of those claiming to identify a moment. stop on the sidewalk to remark how sweet everything smelled. southern regret, my throat aches. that word in particular. what's that face ? it's summer and self-interest spindles its universal center. it's summer and collarbones are all the rage. escape route, the left clavicle. that's mine that's fine with me. I'm a big fan of the clavicle. the fingerboard of the body [the long strip of hard wood over which the strings are stretched]. no score for this. when the alarm sounds, confused, it cannot be Tuesday. the arc of consequence, quite a clumsy utensil. I hear the ruin of all space. those stories make me sad sometimes. a too elaborate penitent gesture—loaned, or you're my theoretic pillow dictionary (abridged). earthshine—its quintessent phases a swan's last arietta, truncated by nature. this final tendril—fractional, there's the rub, the ruin. the rundown sunset : picture perfect, a phrase I have never understood. a face never mumbled. nymphic vision : in my horizon, sins. oblique and laid over everything like onion skin. is there nothing that affords us a genuine reflection ? the world's verticil— its constellations insolent over such misnomers. and every utterance misconceived as a reply. furnished with aspiring heroics, ergo flustered. not still, but again. not Tuesday, you see, because it is too warm and close for Tuesday. outside of this, that is. hollow of the back :

foreign = scary

limitless—angles in the bend of a knee, how many ? the rain early this morning has cleared. low doorways, slanted halls. a brook and crows. this is a very different. strange sleep these days—foreign. a town at the mouth. for regret read. shoulderblades : [traversé les siècles]. feathery adolescent, slim. an egret on an intercoastal. two or three fingers to slip, between. scapular, adolescent secret. sunny, really sunny, and the sound of cows. this could also be true. lingering mood over tea biscuits. how to live suddenly without the everyday. since the walls were filled with new light. since then. since the throat of smoke. lanterns—cruel fiction. I'd like to get it all down but. what worlds luck stumbles upon. "you make these choices"—and bloom in the sidewalk. for egret estuary and rounded stones. skirt nicked in a chain. anecdotal eccentricities. what words lack timbre. [ink saw some wood intelligent enough to get giddiness from a sister] however. we do not live in the center. still. night gives one another's face or voice. the old woman sets and re-sets the table with an extra plate saying "where did all that time go ?" her dinner burned, she pulls the curtains. light stays very late and we land in the alley loose. feet tottering, unbearably heavy. light made the mailboxes, metal—some carelessly open, blue. the knobs of the double doors, also metal, did not easily—the hinges. creak of a place so much larger, or older. and there was singing. "—do not write me long letters." then swallow the coffee, the place, and walk out into a cold night. then walk out of that place into a short fiction of New York. an abstraction of that gesture, or a reasonable facsimile thereof. a short fiction of a view or brick wall or statuary. a sliver fiction of the skin, the rubbery legs. the long walking legs. not still (presupposing continuance) but now (with interruption). we go into the green and just as suddenly we're out. a strange and dark green as though an enormous canvas has abstracted the city. a Tuesday in June, she said "how absurd." what were the chances. to wake knowing outside the skin is that inescapable. mythological to the very last crumbling chunk.

say something geographically accurate. sorcery from the syllogisms. why don't we invert questions in our language ? we suffer the tonic for an elixir. archipelago like an adjective : does the thought re-shape the throat ? the imperfection of our future tense. salvage yard— French verbs in the mouth as a bowl of buttered peas. walking through the chalky white of your reminiscence. and birds picking at trash—nondescript, interesting birds—in a Montreal alley are nothing like childhood blue-sugar-birds on a portico except in the saying-so. hair tucked behind the ear to better understand. fond but not enough : my pity one of the few decorations he took west. people respond to panic, even strangers. particularly strangers. let's interrupt the narrative in the following manner—she parts her lips to curl her lashes and his already are lashes. he opens his mouth to kiss the bluish of her jugular so that his teeth brush the recent dusting. her lashes curled so that she can better make that amazed face. of what happens after I can only tell you little and I'm less sure of what went before. ungainly, so little subtlety in the anonymous seconds. you smoked a cigar. we shared an umbrella. prolepsis melting in a twist of lemon. right as rain behavior, garish with impunity. a flaw, dawn. and rests its sky on my aphoristic sigh. this sometimes sullen city—to exist everywhere and [someone said] stretch being into believing. according to the photographic record : all stairways wrought and turn. your stories make me quiescent. everything sounds like fruit. geographically correct—walking and if there had been a window we'd have only looked through. collected things : breads (two), a three dollar blue chair, (partly) sunny and miscellaneous gears, votive glass—the smell of smoke and soap. cry me a river and throw in a copse of trees. I hear you're expert at cleaning up messes. several failed attempts were made to get her picture while holding a cigarette between her teeth—it is more exciting somehow to think of it between her teeth rather than simply in her mouth. say that again about sunburn, the way deer turn red in summer.

↳ never moving out into

for regret : a hollow in the back. the unfortunate decision to come shaped like an instrument. an adjectival city's eccentricities. a way to feel at home, meals in the same dark bar everyday. a clothesline so we smell like grass in clean laundry. very silent and it was there, too, but silent like long drives or a tea kettle before steam. reading with feet tucked up under you, a transom window. low doorways and everyone would hit their heads eventually. the belly of words is gilt-edged this morning and mist on landscapes parts for footprints. Icarus draws a bath. "conspiring cellos in the swags—" of a moonlet finale. its fingerprint on one blade of grass, or was that me ? there was a promenade missed. I sometimes fear the edifice. wisdom, apocryphal in the jawbone. tourism has its damp wood and cinderblocks. picking dented globes from the garbage and a candle smell of pomegranates embedded in carpet. much like cursory weather, a specter just in peripheral vision. those old-fashioned windows, that resuscitation. an alto clef in twain. in summer we turn and abstractly gesture the universe. better an illogically coherent system. slender and incorrect. and it doesn't matter at all what the boys beyond the tree line are shooting at. the crackle lingers in treble. "may we have the lights please ?" lingers in the sentimental. tranquil—smelting in the meadow's high tide. curator of regret. a re-invented adolescence : foreign sirens through a flawed dawn. the arc of that trajectory unknown. hyacinth arbor— mercurial slip through a tiny aperture. that distracted arc altimetric. as though collidings aren't often mistaken for faith. there were promises made hastily by interrupted clouds and cows lying down in the étude. the celebration off-key, the superstitions stiff with ritual mooring. forgive my long-windedness : but I've no intention of re-initiating correspondence. waxen and staccato, the soothsayer revisits and rains in the after. arias culled from our beautiful conspiracies. our gin vigils, our ears to the rails. a culmination or mosaic sensationally translated to suit the present tense. the usefulness in mistaking myth for faith.

: and rains in the after. orison mediates the skies. waning and adagio, she pauses while undressing for a swim. "stiff with melancholy—" and flickering in the sentiment. gaslights, shattered glass—very toppling atmospheric. claustral—suitable for fusing, refining into silverfish. striking the keys as a mosaic. stretching muscular over the fretwork. there was a willow, a scant brook, a slim cement bridge. vows are kept territorially. your grief matches exactly the paint. angels crook in an elbow. whereby this short fiction [which the chariot race and its thousand satellites made rarely beautiful and intimate with carnival] : a terrazzo chipped and mended with bits of clockfaces. the sorcerer returns and solicits an adolescence—sleep between the shoulderblades. those trophies woven, she pauses. the landscape rolls and yields to water. yields to your gossamer indifference. yes—it makes a beautiful noose. a burden in the hand is worthy of any further number. salvage yard, machine shop—he's forgotten what I take in coffee. not still, but between poses. the rain spindles its macramé, the universe. after all. suspension in approach and retreat, that agonizing orbit. should the tide catch you, swim north or south—never immediately for shore. should you get caught, beware of what you wish for and Greeks bearing gifts. something loyal —a plow, a constellation? the kind of green a hurricane preempts in the afternoon, it gathers. a certainty of innocence, soldered by our concern. and mythological to the last resurgent citation. her latest reincarnation. an antecedent city and its pronominal substitutes. a verb, please? something loyal and muscular to extend. a verb, ambrosic and thick on the lips. to return, a distracted echo. to hoist a saint onto the shoulders. as though the festival doesn't cast a glance and wince at the sidewalk. cullet for our conspiring torches—should the city fall, the walls will remain to mark it. we've written down where we left our shadows, cursory regret—faceless satellites bright with dancing. I have sententious fingers tonight and suffer the tenor, his ellipsis—a tonal translation to suit the presentiment. a pose, a rosary vine.

after all, it's an open letter. a technology of restoration. (he said, perennially boyish). it's either a sawblade or a sunflower. given the mathematics of grief, the variable of an abdomen remains functionally inconstant. a chaotic faith, incorporated—meticulously reproduced in its original glory. technicians of reticence. here, it seems so natural to turn corners that way. pushed and pulled into orbit. antebellum wisteria. there is another language than this. bitter witticisms. oracles, we said, cannot be held accountable for the long term [your rosary of yew-berries] a string of responsibilities, responses in spirit. our reconstruction—charmed, I'm sure. to have sentimental fingers tonight. it's true the raven does not hatch a hawk : stilled by superstition. orison and oracle enact a drama adagio. some loyal oratorio. departmental anguish—mimicking fiction. bemired by girlhood, she pauses for a swim—bluefish and bruises symmetrically his pronouns by proxy. ill with omens, with countless heroic episodes. whose sweet tart blue eyeballs in a bag ? that first half-truth is always a bit of a shock. get out of bed while the steeple's still dappled. sepulchered (your things around my room like relics ?) and disclosed only relatively. disclosed only reluctantly. yet divination requires visibility. equidistant, observant as though the lenses aren't positioned just so. your necessity more silent than mine. a premise concluded hastily in euphemisms. a merle or mottled cluster of dawn pressed to your chest as a scapular. murmur in formal back formation. an abstraction silvered, garbled in jest. integral : theories fail the composition of parts and wholes. martyrologies mistaken for brief emotion. the skin inexorable and operatic. vision fixed prophetic to midheaven—it is indefinite. to read sphere as an action, coiling into sleep. an arching consecrated and still with the weight of its own suspect veneration. weight of early warmth on slate. planed into cozy geometries. the ornamental light-lines expand in openwork curtains from the high window. so much time spirals into these shapes or the ruin of these shapes. here, the corners are a war immobile without your periodic system of streaming inlets.

reluctant to speak freely

without you our arcadian system shakes on a trellis—coiling into speech. what would that prove ? an entire country made of dew and hedgerows. carageen and we realize [all we can really share with people is a taste for the same kinds of weather]. this and that system of despair. as though indifference makes it possible. as though something ugly, a city even, is easier. even in the midst of that precision the fable of waking. what a shame—it all comes truly down to that after all. on the tips of tongues. never the way we speak. if not himself then his ghost. yes—on both your houses, more or less. late night coffee or otherwise and she had figured on indecision— insomniac ambition. she saw experience as text and won the stake for it. no soliloquies now for miles, a gentle sleep tucked under the chin. no soothsaying in full gutters. broke into dialect to express desire—"you have no claim to these" written and erased. as though the difference is a matter of importance and invisibility elicits nonexistence. the flutter of tide water slapped and receded. maybe this isn't what water does. whatever stakes left eddied tremble in my absence. a pleasing vacancy. a dramatic diorama losing tremendous lucidity. that's as it should be—things unwritten are of little interest to archaeologists. a lark no match for a raven. hasty by nature and we've counted on this unreliability, ambiguously ridiculous fallibility. 'in theory' only means I am brave in dreams. the distinction between ravish and ravishing made for a significant footnote. an argument over the profundity of sadness and a trustworthy seawall. should it fall, the unsubmerged land will be awash without demarcation. even at the minute of that precession, decay. its satellites unrequited and salty in the ravelling. in theory—I committed the chance light on buildings, on commons, to memory. commenced ticking off a list of tongueless myths. extant, and incidentally—so much fabric is purely ritual. the kind of air a cloister arranges in clusters and arches. some language barely disguised in retreat. promises rise or faint illumination in crescent phases.

if only someone had undertaken a grammar of forgiveness instead of gumming or chewing at things, wary of the teeth. I committed—as it is, it isn't a bit reflexive. your stories sometimes make me sleep strangely. forlorn—and the cells conspire. "I had a very different body then" and suppose there was an attempt to make a gift of that which was. to give—of course there are lunatics in our street. the only thing to be afraid of is allowing this to become sacred. or another unspeakable. 'unrequited' does not necessarily presuppose the word love nor does it follow that there's anything lovely about it. hindsight objects seem but he knows not seems. someone is snowing. not here, still, but sinking— to the knees but not kneeling per se. Verdi : oh, perhaps it is he ? coincidentally, Chopin is also a chemist in the neighborhood. incidentally, only the heart was buried in Poland. I also have a Copernicus cocktailparty-story and, as a matter of fact, I am just whistling Dixie. this variety catalogued. she wrote the tragedy of hats. she writes that she pretends to live as others do and that he never fails to unlock her door first. some foregone thing : never the way we curl, cathedral. and what is remembered—foolishly (or not) the eyes shut, of course. who was human after all was said and done. in the end this is not a question. (come home please) and what was whispered. I meant, I meant—is varnished. at Delphi or just south of there, its garden squinting white. all of the planets that began as consonants have broken the pact, rendered it useless. the you in morning, closes ("I prefer hours") like watching something die. il y a Ilium. stitched with melioration. lately enamored with the word. commonly, legal memory extends only twenty years—this becomes convenient. your minimal historicism. all of the plans that began as covenants have been given a gloss as adornment. even an interstitial gets nervous. haul of physics, a matter of force or flagstones. the lattice regrets it is not laced. shock is cartoonishly interesting for one second. a (pouring) rainy city is a beautiful excuse to become see-through. there's an air of this about the spire, whisper of ascent.

count clockwise. demarcation : the word dividing the world between beautiful fruits. currents of skeletal realism with a penchant, a general outline—vulnerable, a sketch of a neck. latinization—your minimalist stories make pleasant nonsense. nudes (headless as is their nature) "—begin to crowd the garden." and there's life at sea level to be considered. "the peculiar scaffolding" sculpting a navel, a ribcage, the removal of something missing. frescoes in the transept appear antique, perhaps they are antiquities, fatigued. apply this to our theory of egos and operas. and every measure moving away, the gesture. that's the sound of a thousand industrious insects holding up some gorgeous representation. the aerialist aspires to a law of aesthetics. if not for bias and nostalgia—iota. lotus : disguised as a nightingale gazes at the water. at himself, his grief in the water and so he is many people just then. hurricane's ironwork wrought with verdigris. leaves inside-out the axis. eucalyptus, the esophagus and bury a spoon in the backyard to ward off. superstition strikes a minor chord with you. if all men (in the general sense) were angels, distracted saviors—if, like a deer, you never looked up. [he's posed for me ten thousand times. when he poses I no longer want to recognize him.] condemned and elongated—versant. our gift transliterated. something woeful about new shoes and southern stars—the way they tilt and surrender against the whorl. off-kilter, whatever they tend to resemble. the crux of it : a keel or sail—as though stars, chiselled and cast, could swim that way. proper nouns permit diagnostic service. a kind of nomenclature renovation. an arbitrary city seems inadequate. but this distinguishing basalt —ionic at the delta or mouth. I tried to tell you this more generous translation, etym—ahem. the M7 from Patrickswell from Monasterevin, in absentia. it took that long for the story—still, without that crucial solution. a magpie : prophetic contralto. leaded glass, shadow spheres. at least someone reached for it, a line-drawing of limits. everyone prefers decapitated statues : they consummate promises in haste, without regret. whereas a sluice incurs options and gold.

semaphore down a long off-season beach, your thorny orison ("long-stemmed")
—desire past is only desire of a separate tense. awkward between poses. promise nothing that
could slip through a deadeye. a gravelly duet like a wiser stranger. [ruined garlands a figment
sensible nature bluesilver] shouldn't lightning thus precede thunder in the phrase as well ?
you seem at a loss in your own electricity. not iconic—though I prefer that peculiar
medieval religious blue. smalt, or bluer. the vastness between wish and intent, an account
of betrayal in translation, not its first. someone else's madness in chalk. the mouth closes,
razing the cathedrals. often characterized by an eccentric double voice some found troubling
: 'locutions' or heard language as its own language. a town at the mouth may not be exact.
perhaps it is this fallen city we take with us everywhere. inevitably travelogues are disappointed.
but we've written down where we feasted on its dust. its avenues—apertures : "living silver"
solemnity. questionably furnished. pious ormolu soldered by our consensus. is it apparent—
its significance ? pearl light. as though it isn't often mistaken. its fretwork and orange
orbits, persimmon. infinite, as though a zephyr would weather itself indefinitely within
this : hand-blown glass, webbed, to catch spells. when people would 'have' spells, solstitial.
[given leave—the route, nearly a mountain—over. flight of hawthorn hedges, as though
piercing sleep, comprehending it. permission—the route, scenic : filled with signs for
tourists perhaps down footprints to sleep (in Latin *somnus*, here *yours*) leave to extract—
as in 'to wake' very nearly—peat (really) in the hollow, the breastbone tomorrow morning.]
a place, a color he had never seen—merely imagined. like the clavichord and think
of all the things you wish were never un-learned. transmuted to suit something larger. alembic
ebb etching. make-believe skies water-stained, tidal marshes—remember. pages suddenly
fabled. sleeping syllabic, heretic. he does not see her (disguised as a figment) but a re-
translation, not exact ("loosely adapted"). all horizons on our heads : woeful and empty the sea.

the charm (in trees ? windows ?) of finches or a confused orphéon, our maudlin concern. etymologies do not take us one step closer to or farther from the 'truth' of her hair—*parapleureuse* : having known too much of water. votives in unction jars. the vestibule of intention, secular and yet pressed to the chest. or just as well Hansel and Gretel, of a kind, smiling their ridiculously false Paris. an hysterical Paris where, were trains different things, I nearly could have espied you once. trains being what they are—"cry me au revoir" and allow the drowning to drown (what little throat framed that note ?). what language we wrestle on the head of a pin—its ecliptics and lenitions make all but the weather mysterious to me. no, even that. flaxen and detached, she postures directions for repentance : enter, at last, sola. whatever ghostly coves. rhythmic histories we cannot help but hear. echo now, sleep, mourn and even—the gods by-passed where only genuflections are heir. fortifications for a beguilement. begin. the surprise sadly wrecked, we land loose in the alley. of course, lunatics and sterling silver operatics. sculpting an umbrella, plainly. some thing articulate in its ruination. at the time, it didn't seem very important. will the walls now be filled or fallen ? into fiction. and how much more can it hold, a staggering plinth. maps created, that face, for my benefit were not geographically accurate. and perhaps there isn't another. so much surrender, fixation. in this hemisphere I have seen you, I have been episodic. ruminate—an antonym of gesture. the birds and trees, living, presented a cinematic paradox no one had prepared for in back and white. and 'north' is just as baffling and imaginary as anything else. as though to say it is true eliminates this. he follows the voice, its scales onto the sidewalk hoping to find it where he wants it and does. placement is determined, after all, by relation to nonharmonics. rash wingspan and green—vowel-like vibrations. yes—we have that between us, and that too. they could otherwise be seen as things in common. ashes, ash-*ling*. even(song)—according to the legend, things close.

my lengthy exits make you nervous. patient to a fault—the road narrows and it rains harder. this never fails and why should it ? the neighborhood without an umbrella is foreign. seriously, perhaps too much so because the day is delightfully sentimental. nothing understands how it works and it's better that way. sunken replication-relief : three graces. adorned, in a strange fashion then, with intemperate fish. "it looks like they're swimming too." maybe to you. in eden or elsewhere. it could be paradise since everything's relative. our selves [did not bite to the core of the apple], acrobats. forest street, not really an alley but thin with taxis that evening (what it will be like when the lights—). let me know if you—. till then—. explain something simple. the way even though eyes are closed one can tell they're looking upward. look closely ("I prefer hers"). tonight, provoked by arias, you will glance at a sprite 'over-the-shoulder' again. atmosphere supercedes sentiment, suspension. panic arrives with the first anchorage and words revert to signs. moonshine, periodic occultation. sense, albeit multiple, gently cupped in your hand. our street and streets where we have never lived lined with brownstones, their tiled kitchens. eavesdropping, jealous—that thin evening and collarbones. you said—now (suddenly) you understood why people have painted nudes for centuries ("like a mountain")—après l'opéra (detail). living that is to live already with ashes. [the book is a mystery whose only merit is to be open on her thighs.] a gasp, surprised, as though the outcome isn't known better than legend permits. every morning for seventy years he played Bach. with you, it's Wagner : high tide affection for a jetty. I dreamt— they were onstage again, the one with the white elysium-light backdrop, but she had become so tiny that he put her in his mouth—and woke confused. it seems I have already left many times under suspicion of that skyline. were there another, if only there were. rue may be an avenue and fennel a divining rod, the rowhouses frowning with crows. [if all our eyes had the clarity of apples] if gilded our clairvoyant age could not be chosen or duplicated or pronounced.

penultimate turn of the hourglass. I can never seem to get away from it. misericorde. Ithaca's gorges. let bygones be, a wild relief. hue and cry. memory or memorized—there are miles. smidgen, sand, and aperture. openwork geometrics, columnar orders. magister-lantern : that's how it's done. a pinhole, smoke, mirrors. something has to happen—nothing will come of nothing. at this point, roads seem ridiculously overdone and the mapmakers cross their fingers. all of this is slept through, even the steeple is chaste. pre-overture : discordant, delectable grief that raises the hair on my neck, leaning forward. orchestrations— implying deliberate. palaces, prisons, prisms : more of the same. musculature, his mathematical shoulderblades. sleep could be less paradox, more pedentive and its lyrically adjacent arches. some with a caul, you—a clockface. just born, I'd have been afraid to hold you. nouns and nostalgia sewn into your pockets, hems, safekeeping. if we wore light, movement, as film does. reasonable doubt and sensible horizons. so they say, he was found on the Holy Rosary steps with his violin. something about the last streetcar across. the one with the wings made of hangers and twine. the one with the immortality ode. the anatomy of immortality. faithful meridian. hinter, a grace note : sunlight through clouds. for regret— sentience. Lir's daughters on the ocean floor absurdly taking their tea. shrines and silences. the sand moving, beach replenishment. arpeggio, to disappear as if by melting. church-bells visible from but unheard in the nursery. tolling, crowning (a well-tempered clavier). we agreed, they could not duplicate it—not even in cafés and obsessive boxes. the theater of suitcase. is the truth about little girls and comets the trap with you too ? *vide* : the slope of the neck in distress and slender, distinguishing it from the goose. dear bleuet, that hurts the way the roots of hair can hurt. his daughters taking to salt, sea-struck. iota : locus. and no more was heard of her though a wild belief claimed she'd sing. that's what it is to vanish, folkloric. striking the keys as a mosaic. a gorgerin (fallen with stone). I remain, sincerely—

geography anatomized : the girl unfinished. pre-nuptial and acrylic, all sins carefully accounted for—a moment on pins and needles. and every Wednesday night the ritualized numbness. low doorways, slanted halls, the branching nightmare of a child too aware. coiling on a trellis, carageen. ergo, our opera theory. out of the chaotic variety of what was possible— here is what was, what "had to happen." in-spite-of-myself but myself, transfusion. there is no night—miscellanea resulting in an irrelevant and chronic case of historiography. arguments ensued, our generic argument with several accessible spaces for plugging in specifics. hidden in heather and gorse (isn't that how it's meant to go ?) when the sea shall give up. this vicious circle stuck stuttering its heroics—his art is a grammar that appeals to me. the untillable landscape of a sternum, elsewhere. enumeration of articles. an apple of available discretion. the edge of an assassin and I have put on my best face. biography as a system of betrayals (this from someone who has never claimed to be an optimist). with girlish courage she assures us that she walks in the sky. hanging harps of discord in an alphabet of trees, leaves. this was done to ease memorization, this was done by design—if design could be accidental. that the incidental becomes instead central. the skirmish between figurehead and figurine has been revived. agonies cameo in threes. I left quite unconcerned but (and this is clearly the most important point) second-guessed thoroughly at a later date. a bridge falling down with bells on. yes—she looks remarkably well for one who hasn't blinked in a decade or more. and ever this omen. an utterance against interest, hysterically inadmissible. if that isn't proper dinner-table conversation—the wholly felt will be surgically removed. with the approach of fabled fair weather, we grow accustomed to long walks. either in common or individually—camouflaged by fragrant thickets. consider the effort a lullaby : say goodnight goodnight several times to insure comprehension, reciprocation, which defeats the purpose. past the picturesque shipwreck, a river no one notices except to cross despite its tidal pools, eddies—if ominous then intricate. another morning, soft rushed to wake where east is to our west. rivaled, I but an anapest. partial to waltzes, we are mathematically incompatible. since I cannot be sure *if* I certainly cannot say *why*. out of the chaos of what happened, this is what surely will happen. again, we endure long years. separation : she drags a train of it. chandeliers, baroque in exile. in a larger philosophy than the one to which I aspire, or from the French 'to hope' or 'to put trust in'—to wish, rivulets. for something industrial amidst extensive and literate clouds. if she unmask to the moon, leaded transoms. an instrument for taking—in time-honored tradition. as though that wasn't proof enough. tolling ex cathedra, boning of the neck. threaded—a web or way out, either. Héloïse, your feathers choke me. crowded skyline stories. a desire to be renowned for stillness yet she is manifested perpetually in grievous motion. while absent-minded singing is the most comforting sound—if nothing brightens soon I'll take my librettos and go home. its skin romantic-sized : melancholy anatomized. an elaborate penance for having been that girl. literally *for what* not *why*—her jetty amulet fallen weep a garland for a brook. torn in tatters, apropos. black, pink, oil-lily blue alternate in wakes and shake fog from your hair. something secret between, inappropriate but not terribly so. this is where it begins—within the ellipse. that's the way, always. astrolabe : a pen and spindle. this is a woman smoking. these are your nervous fingernails. this is a delicious salad, a cold night, a long walk home. your mad kings and sad stories—crowded, filmy. follow me into the desert—despite or because of your crooked mouth. heard in camera, and happily ever after. agonist, alive inside this. here, almost everyone is marked by that cloudy, classically iconographic radiance. relax, it may rain any minute now. the consonance that results. an arc as finite representation, restoration of that which was better left rundown. much original charm : dormers, moldings, curtail steps (origin unknown). should you need me in the dark, descend with care.

gun moll complex (or a loose adaption thereof). chance-medley of signs, chorus lines. wc go into the white but it moves along like weather. I asked if there was motive—not necessarily if it was ulterior. every dusty constellation made pretty for the event. reproduction of the infinite within finite space, the ruin. grand operatic gestures. today the unrealized possibility of opening windows. five tangled horizons on a very, very fine-toothed comb. I told no one : regardless, there wasn't a viable translation or explanation. and there she will be shriven—noted in the text. perpendicular and center interchanged, misplaced. the appearance was that of a woman who had walked quite far in the rain. at sunset or high tide : there were bagpipes on the beach. this is true. although, obviously, other lonely phenomena could be as well. suffused, an influx of gaslight. another glass of birthday moonshine. fraught with the mystic, handwritten. things collected : but these are not really ours. the city woke without its skin which resembles an attempt to capture the love story of near-saints on film. one of my favorite brilliant failures. a limitless vice shamelessly admitted. fascination with hatpins. the ground opens arms. when the cloister stones were disassembled and given new homes—all the medieval fell away. heretical dress and token placement. my life-long dread of spider-eyes and other façades. desperate, despite your eloquent arguments to the contrary, remains contentious. something about its shape, its shadow—an excerpt meant as a treaty. the fragment is more than a snag. an unrecognized musical phrase crosses the street. festooned with respite—sorcery for the sleepless. reasons will escape us. even the simplest avenues cannot be kept straight. the orange afternoon and the date on paper. our surroundings weren't fooled. for eros—heroics. I, too, have been. there must be another point of departure. upon returning—a melody, a ricorso on a spinet. shored against regret. and then another departure : an exact echo resounding. thick chords preferred. there must be something bittersweet to it : the tongue won't have it any other way.

half-sentence on the lip and for months what would have been that night. doubly unreal—it is not night. not yet, or still. this system derived from essentially undefined points and lines : your feverish indeterminacy. heaven stolen and other things rendered. I suspect dreaming a hand on the neck, heaviness aside. let's be suspicious. this is very suspicious, is good broken music. a sentiment often misunderstood : I do not want anything to happen, only the right to regret what does not. something singular and famished and others drawn by loss. beautiful, and meant as freighted with every possible problematic definition. and she arrives with scissors and a smile. a ritual eventually overtook—in popularity due to its simplicity and pocket accessibility. you choose your mysteries with care—each maiden suffrage Dymphna with a willow. never by the book : "if only for the frontispiece— which is good only as long as this weather holds." observe that I never sit properly but 'perch' (there is the small matter of my fee). it has all been done and that repetition and easeful clicking became exactly the point. as to what remains. it remains in that choked manner of speaking with smoke in the throat, strict reciprocity. with very selective historical affections. each moveable feast, its new moon calculations. today's manufactured scenery—four-walled open air, terraces, intermissions, richly anonymous. what magic forgot or have I a heart for it ? spiny, dejected umbrella. every one imposed upon another, the other upon one and so on until we call it a day. delay before us in station. brightly night fishing. my street ready with its ashes, emblematic. our own auto-da-fé. because I do not live at the end, walking home I see, but never reach, water. abalone : ear-shaped and prescient. ornamental in the form of a box with every color of the southern afternoon's wane. she has a word for this—it's archaic. superstition proposes it is drawn by dancing, hereafter set down on the knees. escape wheel and anchor do not sanctify but provide periodic impulses. aware of relative dangers [flock to them for the main grace of their gravities] I've had about enough of these lousy winter potatoes.

our knowledge of how to build vaults is not theoretical. miraculously, a long life despite all the sharp instruments, the hoarded mirrors. not quite capable of faithful reflection. advised against this in the evening—when one is more easily given to interminable weeping. furthering the misconception [with the belated and meaningless tenderness of her own] perpetuates willful misinterpretation. technique of illumination : vestal vellum. this crisis of arithmetic is this : vacillation, toward the opposed and return. I look, I cannot look, I cannot help but look (there is some doubt as to the authenticity of this correspondence). the crispier, the colder it is—the more realistic we seem from a distance. an object of memory to close your fingers around or dangle from a watch-chain. the magpie : prophet of loss. deprived of the actual experience. it's neither here not there, aisling. "it is always a matter, my darling." another maroon station wagon, another beheaded virgin. she had a dream in which a long purple string issued from her mouth—she made a ball of it. there is no 'definitive text,' then. for regret : poor circulation or the consonance that results. low relief indeed. were they statisticians or seraphim, we'd have something to discuss. rhetoric to which I am profoundly indifferent. if any map is truly useless, outdated—demurely flinching these terracotta statuettes. I give it up, it's already past due. the city in every invisible language in the cross-hairs of the window. its shadow squarely on your forehead. spindled ricorso of return and return : the plaintiff's reply to the defendant's rejoinder. asked what I felt, I volunteered what I thought instead. is that ticking an endearment ? anecdotal notice that of late she prefers the odd phrase : "say I" and it was observed that this must be an insistence to speak so often of herself. free from local magnetic influence. strings that either double or replace one or more voices. there is your crucial unravelling. and for those who rush down the stairs—counting to three. so say I agree. a collection of madrigals dressed as castles : uttering and helpless to the elements, known and unknown. I insist on you.

where the limbs join each other—laid flat. a memento of the area between arriving and parting. fiction, surrender. where once there was reason the corners are turning from my own frightened voice. my own frightening voice toward the sidewalk and the dark rain cars (once that sound was a child sent to bed early, the ocean near enough). that was a boy falling from a tree, everyone said so. here now as it was painstakingly scripted only to be a failure of improvisation, already existed. falling in a most "carefully careless" arc—sculpted from cutlery above a place to rest. mistaken, hairs tangled and staticked from the vulgate primer. from this particular vantage everything is made of angles and so immediate—sudden and incoherent. chemical mysteries bookmarked in pockets. and grow calmer. the hands quieter (less like feathers). more like machinations for the banishment of all constructed to suit. that's my name the way you write it : recognizably guised. reeling when the sound stopped, resigned. I am going to have to learn how to look at you. what I like best is its uncomfortable truth. the crackling the results from such insulated accumulation. equilibrium inherent to stationary bodies. before they are irreversibly cast. this dispensed with the typical caveats. stone so easily grows accustomed. cut and cut again, cut over and over we find the seal much stronger than its skin. when the widow turned to granite my face was quite burned by the sun —but only that. tough exposure. though you would rather her all quartz. tyrranical genetics. that's the smile at your most ambiguous. that's desire smiling itself into doubt, throwing its voice. that's magnetics at a loss, absented taxis. a southern light : if you paint your face again you'll disappear. ribs vaulted so that centering is reduced. ideas collapse into border vignettes. in your hands with abandon, backing away. did I do that or did you do that ? implore and obscure share similar roots. it was dark (small dome light) and a fault fell between, bewildered by so many exquisitely put questions. "speaking from the belly" and with this squarely, our shoulders. fixity, fixity. yes—that is an accurate reflection of the time. and still waits that way.

alphabet of houses along a canal. and the alphabet of tools that made and unmade them. this evening a masterpiece of thievery—unrequited satellites. the mouth closes a museum of light. how has the supple become anonymous ? tenderly flinching, noticing motive and a foolishness I'm prepared to live with. if it be cinematic, or system—night my foreign life. intention toward devotional sentiment. byzantine crosshatch (whiskey lipped)—unmoored by it. no desire without the ventriloquism of desire or a lexical substitute for it. outside of this, that is. equidistance, our elliptics. work out that susceptibility to orphic glances. learn to stay away. lean in talking to the way you breathe. that's a science of heredity, not fate. it could be called coincidence if I believed in them, or learned to say less. my sign, so he tells me, is dissolution. a foolishness I'm not unfamiliar with. having scrubbed the glasses free of sediment, having swallowed the timepiece whole and regular. so often hypocrisy is mistaken for martyrdom. here is your first shining crisis letter. paint the face, that way again : eerily adult. the landscape is a lie once we go outside, it hasn't been altered at all. and their demands unfurl at you. cellophane pressed with ogham, other scratches. requiem half-masted. your isolation exactly the disused bandshell—holding its shape. little else these days is so efficient and extraordinarily considerate. there's my emotional cue. that close—but no closer. physical reaction to a forgotten vernacular. a mouth greedy for rest. there's no slow start to legs spidery on the steps. fragments of a lover's iconography. we also survive in knowing that knowing less is not a way out of being obliged to be in the world. as un-indicted co-conspirators, our responsibilities have artificially immunized consequences. note : for decorative purposes only, sand is not calibrated. as it's neither paginated nor foliated, this miniature will serve as urge. yes—that's marvellously logical. a manifest distrust even in the face of it. though whorled in peculiar blue at our creation. tempera where meant to obscure. certainly manmade. encircled by meridians and other senseless measurements.

the most vulnerable room—eiderdown for nightmares. domesticity evident in every window : lit, unlit. rigid crescendo of sincerity and symmetry, marching on with grimly determined tenderness. I'd have rather been still and unsaid. sometimes the margins are awry, flirting at edges. he said "burn the books" and was exempted in disassembly. enlistment of disasters. in all their formal, caramelized majesty. that house is only a meta-of home. and no matter how often we listen—it's still a race for the strings to catch the bells, it's a desire for coincidence. miraculous rather than clever. the effort, it's tangled in your fingers. declare weary end to drama. dressed for surrender and verbatim. stretched to span a full octave, some thing doesn't begin, something else begins. likewise variable. how long can I reasonably expect to go without saying. answered in abstractions at the base of our spines. and another go at social, reproduced by kind permission. someone will step out into a foreign city and learn it. other anniversaries, they pass and I detest the semi-precious. a minor fissure, pointedly without direction : devotion as diversion. vice versa—the difference is inexplicable. neatly pressed and self-consciously irrelevant. an eighth note : as pictorial idiom, gradual with the ordinary. vellum leaves flat under glass. on the gallery floor with your graph paper. we can make anything routine as it happens and redoubles. becomes hysterical and archival. a short while will drag me up from your face in small rooms. all that turnpike. amazingly precise in its momentariness yet distrusted due to that exact feature. in a few blocks the frescoes will squint the sun in their eyes and mind the clocktower. she warned me that unwashed dishes cause insomnia. the girl pauses, storm doors slam and memento moored. this gesture presently before the body—similar in every example. failing the mouth, hands will want for occupation and crisscross the torso. glances and hair down, their bodies produce no sound. yards of illusion hang from skinny frames. basilicas diminish, echoes diminish, and the saints are restored their sight. consider this mirror like motion. still and unsaid, dazzled to death.

PATTIE MCCARTHY co-founded and edits BeautifulSwimmer Press. She received her MA from Temple University and is the author of two chapbooks, *Octaves* and *Choragus*. This is her first full-length collection. Her work has appeared in many journals and magazines, including *The Boston Review*, *Facture*, *ixnay magazine*, *Kenning*, *Outlet*, *Poets and Poems* on the St. Mark's Poetry Project Website, and *The Transcendental Friend*. She currently teaches at Towson University and Loyola College in Baltimore.